Samo Kreutz

No Bigger Than a Crumb

Cyberwit.net
HIG 45 Kaushambi Kunj, Kalindipuram
Allahabad - 211011 (U.P.) India
http://www.cyberwit.net
Tel: +(91) 9415091004
E-mail: info@cyberwit.net

Printed in India at VCORE CONNECT LLP.

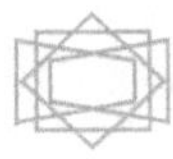

*p*erfume bottle
well preserved in it
bird tunes

First ascent to the sun

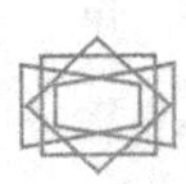

*f*ascinated boy
the first ascent to the sun
from his dad's shoulders

*o*čaran fantič
prvi vzpon proti soncu
z očkovih ramen

*b*aby in a cradle
waking up a wide smile
the mother's steps

*m*aple syrup
her naughty smile
golden

*m*ass of vehicles …
each one of them distributes
its own dawn

*s*tanding by the window
all the street sounds
inside me

young woman
shared with a stranger
her fragrance

new morning
closest to the sun
me and the old trees

city library
on shelves with books
the abundance of sun

blacksmith workshop
in the master's hands
sparrow chirrup

robust fortress
everywhere outside
spring

magnolia tree
hanging on a branch
a girl's whisper

enjoyable sunshine
flourished with primroses
young love

cocoon …
for the first time
she becomes a mum

snowdrops
so much whiter
his memories

widow
keeping her company
the scent of daffodils

small garden
planted in all beds
granny's presence

walking the dog
no longer on a leash
playfulness

*s*oft pitter-patter
my daydreaming
gone

*j*ob interview
flawlessly performed
a sparrow's song

*d*elightful sun
starting to blossom
his career

working in a field
abundantly manured
farmer's shadow

clean laundry
smelling so pleasant
wind from the stable

giant pear tree…
up and down the ladder
bird melodies

*s*afely arrived
without any postage stamp –
the wren's chirping

*o*ne little kiss
now her mother too
smells like a flower

*b*utterfly in a palm
gently carried around
my father

*d*azzling petals
a walk around the trees
virtual

*h*is old neighbourhood
talking like grown-ups
the other boys

*b*usker rests
new leading player
the steady breeze

*m*ystery novel
catching the breath
me and the wind

*r*eshaping
the wrinkles on her face –
red carnation

*s*pring water
never tasted better
the clouds

*g*entle breeze
letting go
a secret

*a*pril drizzle
even her scars
caressed

*e*arly spring rain
looking for a shelter
the mist

open fence gate
coming to the yard
midday downpour

plantain syrup
calming his bad cough
a taste of rainbow

river rapids
still so many things
unspoken

*f*alling
just to live inside me
cherry blossoms

*t*asting so strange
this dandelion salad –
a widowhood

*s*ky gazing
no special star found
a fatherless child

*p*uddle…
between him and her
the whole moon

*f*ormer inn
sparrows in front of it
quench their thirst

бivša gostilna
pred njo utaplja žejo
kopica vrabcev

In a stupendous outfit

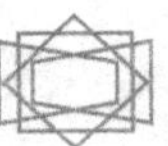

overgrown weeds
a half-rotten stump
full of greenery

razraslo ščavje
že napol preperel štor
spet poln zelenja

dry branch
fluttering around it
baby's first words

*c*olourful meadow
blooming profusely
exhilaration

*o*ld lady on the bus
sharing a seat with her
lavender scent

*w*orn suitcase
neatly folded in it
the smell of home

*a*thletic track
running side by side
me and the summer

*c*ity market
early morning sun
already there

*c*lassroom…
in front of the blackboard
the begonia scent

pretending
to be bigger than us –
a cat on the roof

dandelion seeds
desire for a brother
near the sun

megapolis…
staring at the potted plant
a screensaver deer

light snack
enriching my slice of bread
the magnolia scent

his first drawing…
already a masterpiece
in mum's eyes

boys' ripped jeans
a freedom I once knew
now too tight

*d*ried carnation
so many promises
unfulfilled

*f*ather's notes
still a mystery to me
his handwriting

*c*leaned apartment
coming for a visit
a cat

black ants
brought into my home
the smell of peonies

dazzling sun…
extremely benignant
a face on election poster

yoga lessons
I become one
with a mosquito

crossroads …
a bumblebee leads me
into my inner self

year of a tiger
all the courage needed
to invite her out

rendezvous …
more talkative as he
the rose fragrance

wedding day
in a stupendous outfit
flowering pear tree

tropical island
on vacation with me
the sun

restless sea
heavily deluged
a bird shadow

*r*eflection in the river
the sun and the clouds
all over her face

*t*hought of youth
pattering on a porch
a soft wind

*s*ummer solstice
meeting with a friend
nostalgic

*g*oing to the doctor
suddenly so heavy
tiny raindrops

*t*orrent
in hundreds of pieces
me and the sky

*h*awk's cry
a mighty river
meandering

*b*luebird on a tree
raised at least a little
storm clouds

*h*idden meadow
not so fragrant as once
the grass

*n*ightingale
too small for its singing
darkened woods

*l*ate summer forest
I try not to disturb
falling leaves

*p*olished shoes
all shadows on them
perfectly cleaned

zloščeni čevlji
brezhibno očiščene
vse sence na njih

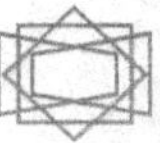

Wildlife voices

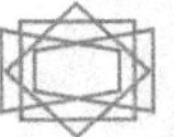

*f*ortune cookie
no bigger than a crumb
the sun on her plate

*b*aby in a bassinet
sleeping peacefully
the future

*p*iškotek usode
nič večje kot drobtina
sonce na pladnju

parents' bedroom
carefully straighten up
father's silence

morning fog
still recognizable
children's laughter

dreary day
changing my perception
hot chicken soup

*t*oddler's room …
in her teddy bear's old eyes
still a girl

*a*utumn meadow
a boy among the grasses
a late bloomer

*p*ears picking
between me and wasps
a struggle for every fruit

church service
heavily disturbed
a dust

sound of the sea
a quarrel next-door
drowned

high tide
finally reaches the stars
a dried leaf

*s*eeding thyme …
immediately strengthened
my inner child

*b*ird hunter
carried around in a bag
wildlife voices

*t*op of the Triglav
already outside Slovenia
my thoughts

lichen on stone
a haiku beneath it
green

boarding a plane
in a passenger cabin
rowan leaf

group of pilgrims
too small for all the pleas
a church

thick smog
a man and chickadee song
equally blurred

different city
but all the worries
still the same

refugee camp
planted in a nearby field
shadows of the tents

*a*sylum home
seeking for the child
a velvet teddy bear

*c*limate summit
people and the murk
face-to-face

*d*eserted cottage…
those days I wasn't afraid
to dream

*b*asket of mushrooms
left in the woods
their faint scent

*t*orrential rain
much different sounds
my cv for a job

*h*er silent words
paused for a moment
autumn downpour

church interior
kneeling on the floor
yellow leaf

christening…
at the baby's bare head
the nest of a rainbow

book club meeting
the life I never lead
so familiar

closed gallery
secret Monet's admirer –
a ladybug

mammoth skeleton
fragments of skin on it
a spiderweb

autumn evening
I share my late lunch
with the crow's cry

*g*rand tidying
clean from head to toe
a quietness

*f*alling star…
shifting the position
a stray dog

*a*dorable baby
absent at his birth
this blue moon

*r*oom in the dark
walking unobstructed
a child's fantasy

*s*ilent movie
another conversation
with teenage daughter

*s*hadow lamp
deer head on a wall
alive

*w*edding night
embedded in her ring
the moonshine

*t*his apple tree…
all the attempts to capture
a constellation

*s*tarry evening
my face in the window
the new universe

quiet splashes
trying to slip away
the sturgeon moon

abstract painting   abstraktna slika
the only identifiable   edino razpoznaven
a beetle on the frame   hrošč na okvirju

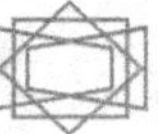

A boy's lost shoe

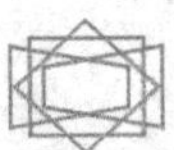

*m*odel of a castle
occupying the whole hill
a boy's cap

*m*aketa gradu
celoten hrib zaseda
dečkova kapa

*c*hildren's room
all the shadows in it
disordered

*m*orning star …
covering it completely
a dinosaur toy

*b*ounce music
dancing all around
a moth

*s*mall spider
its shadow in the corner
wallpaper last detail

baby airplane kit
years long gone
return

father's photo
coming out of his room
the morning light

winter begins
no place in my notebook
for revised resolutions

*t*hick ice crust
preserved for latter
spoors

*S*unday Mass
leaving a half-empty church
a sermon

*a*bandoned warehouse
left on the rusty shelves
the workers' voices

cold rain
staying inside
even my gaze

muddy road
greyish and all wet
a child's reflection

flood devastation …
his contemptuous words
one too many

*h*unting area
no more in the line of fire
light wind

*c*old wave
coming from afar
deep silence

*s*nowdrift
hidden at least a little
her loneliness

*i*cy puddle
playing with a child
rainbow and clouds

*b*lizzard alert
new thirty inches
of worries

*f*reezing cold
in my shadow's hug
a snowman

slush ice
slightly changed
just the quietness

winter sunset
with me on the street
the warmth of a home

power outage...
illuminating the city
snow patches

*r*aising the hands …
I let the stars to touch
moon mount

*G*reat Bear reflection…
bringing him safely back
the cat's eyes

*N*ew Year…
no different as before
his snoring

*s*culpting …
her inner demons
clayed

*e*arthquake
shaking most noticeable
a void in the mirror

*c*emetery …
at its final resting place
a robin's warble

exodus…
waiting for the train
a boy's lost shoe

end of the attack
rescued from the ruins
plush elephant

konec napada
rešen izpod ruševin
plišasti slonček

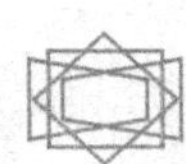

A WORD OR TWO ABOUT THE AUTHOR

Samo Kreutz lives in Ljubljana, Slovenia. He began to write as an eight-year-old boy, when he wrote his first story (and later a poem). One day his parents told him that simply by writing he cannot earn enough for a decent life, so he replied that he will become a writer and a joiner. Now, at the age of forty-seven, he is not yet a joiner (nor a carpenter), but the Bachelor of Economics, who besides poetry and short stories, also writes novels and haiku (since 2011). He is the author of ten books in Slovene (all published by the Ekslibris, publishing house in Ljubljana) and two in English (they are haiku books, one is titled

The Stars for Tonight, and the other is *A Time Different from Ours*, both published by Cyberwit.net). His work has appeared in various Slovenian literary magazines, anthologies, on national Radio, on several international websites, e- and printed journals (most recently in the *Jalmurra: Art & Poetry Journal* and in the *Green Ink Poetry*).

A NOTE ABOUT THE BOOK

No Bigger Than a Crumb consists of 155 haiku. The poems in this collection are about us (our greatness, as well as smallness), and the influence we have on other people's lives. They are joined by those with a touch of nature, and thus forming the contrast. The majority of these haiku can be found (in English, Slovene or both versions) in printed journals: *Better Than Starbucks: Poetry and Fiction Journal, Kingfisher Journal, Seashores: Haiku Journal,* and *Taj Mahal Review,* on websites: *Akita International Haiku Network, Ariel Chart: international literary journal, Asahi Haikuist Network, Autumn Moon Haiku Journal, Cold Moon Journal, Creatrix Haiku and Poetry Journal, Dwelling Literary, First Literary Review – East, Green Ink Poetry, Ink Sweat & Tears: The poetry and prose webzine, Jalmurra: Art and Poetry Journal, Locutio, Poetry Pea, Stardust Haiku Online Journal, The Bamboo Hut, The Big Windows Review, The Haiku Foundation (Haiku Dialogue), The Heron's Nest,* and *Wales Haiku Journal,* in anthologies: *Haiku zbornik: Ludbreg, Pesem si: zbornik, Samoborski haiku susreti Darko Plažanin,* and in quite a few broadcasts on the national Radio.

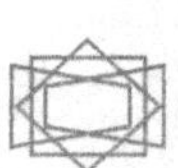

CONTENTS

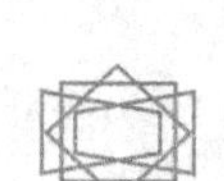

9 789390 601899